The Birth Famine

The Birth Famine

If No Children, Then No Future

MICHAEL CHARLES MASTER
Author of *Save America Now!* and
Rules for Conservatives.

ISBN: 1507898681
ISBN 13: 9781507898680
Library of Congress Control Number: 2015902456
CreateSpace Independent Publishing Platform
North Charleston, South Carolina

Introduction

"*Rules for Conservatives*" and "*Save America Now*" were written by me to expose the root causes to the problems facing America and to offer possible solutions. Both of those books proposed that children are the future for America. American citizens are not making enough children. America is in a birth famine. So the future of America is at risk.

Some people will object to the use of terms like vagina and penis. Some might object to describing what happens during an abortion. Some will allow their political bias to interfere with their ability to analyze facts without prejudice. And some will be defensive about the comments about feminists or businessmen or God or Jews or evolution or gays or immigrants. Yes, I understand how those people feel. My own wife and daughter felt just like that about discussing many of those topics. But you will find that those are the topics that need to be discussed if we want to correct the birth famine in America.

The USA needs a growing population of citizens to have a growing economy. That requires more than 2 children per woman to eliminate any need for immigrants. The average birth rate to American citizens is much lower than 2 per woman. Because of this birth famine to American citizens, the average age of American citizens is increasing. The long term viability of Social Security is questionable as fewer young citizens pay into the system than the number of people who are retiring from the work force. Average medical costs per capita are increasing as an older society needs more medical care than a younger one. The economy is contracting as an older society buys fewer products like housing, cars, and "stuff" that make for a robust economy.

Even though some politicians discuss the over-population problem in the world, all political leaders in the USA want to increase the USA population. Otherwise, why would they continue to encourage more immigrants to come to America? The immigrants increase consumption of products in the USA and provide low paid and/or high skilled workers who offset the effects of the low birth rate of American citizens. So politicians and businessmen want more immigrants to come to America.

Fewer American citizens are getting married, so a comparison of birth rates for families is irrelevant. And the government hides the fact that it includes births to immigrants who are having lots of children when it publishes the annual birth rate for America. When a comparison is made about births per American women citizens, the birth rate has fallen by at least 2/3 to a level that is less than half of the 2.1 children per woman that is needed to sustain the population of citizens in the USA. Without immigration and the births of children to immigrants in the USA as "anchor babies," the USA would be shrinking in population. Massive immigration increased welfare costs, increased crime, and increased costs for government supplied benefits like healthcare and education. As immigrants competed for jobs, wages decreased for American workers. Of even greater concern is that the soul of America, the values of our founding fathers, is slowly being destroyed by too much immigration (legal and illegal).

A long-time friend of mine, Paul, argued with me that the low birth rate for citizens is irreversible. Having fewer children has become part of the culture. He added that the economic costs of living in the USA require that most families to be two income families to realize the "American dream," which leaves them little time to raise children correctly, if at all.

Well, the average American citizen certainly owns much more "stuff" and does much more "stuff" than the average Americans of 50 years ago. So the scenario by Paul about the American dream must mean that young people want to acquire more stuff and do more stuff than their parents did ... which requires two incomes per family at the expense of having children.

Others claim that the poor economy of 2009 helped cause the low birth rate. That is just not true. The decreasing birth rate to USA citizens started in the 1970s, long before the recession of 2009. And the birth rate has decreased during good times and bad times. So a poor economy is not the reason for a low birth rate. Greed is the reason. Stuff and life styles are more important than raising children. The recession of 2009 was caused by the low birth rate in the 1970s. The recession of 1960s was caused by the deaths of 500,000 young men in WWII of the 1940s. Politicians are well aware how the demographics of people between the ages of 20 and 60 affect the economy the most, how the births of 40 years ago affect the economy of today, yet they do nothing to fix the current birth famine and its affect on the future.

Another friend of mine, (Catholic) Father Tim, made this comment to me: as a society becomes more educated, other things become more important to it than raising children. So how smart is such a society that places immediate attainment of things as more important than the future, even if it is well educated? Evidently, being educated does not mean being smart.

Those comments from Paul and Father Tim motivated me to write this book. This book is about children and their importance to the future.

Children are the future. Without enough children, there is no future. Without children, life will end.

The low birth rate of American citizens is going to be the demise of America. And then if there is too much immigration to offset the low birth rate, there will be no American culture as we know it today. The expenses to assimilate those immigrants will be much too high. The soul of America will be destroyed. If no children, then no future.

Since the release of my books "Save America Now" and "Rules for Conservatives," Harry Dent released his book "The Demographic Cliff," published by the Penguin Group in 2014. It comes to the same conclusion as my books that the low birth rate to American citizens is catastrophic for America. Mr. Dent independently noticed so many of the same issues as me ... Harry Dent from statistics and me by intuition. It is interesting that each of us used some of the same comparisons independently ... like the use of the four seasons to explain the stages of income and consumption in a person's life as a person ages.

Please understand that the birth famine can be reversed. The governments (federal, state, and local) can implement programs like those presented at the end of this book to help increase the birth rate. With enough children, there will be a future. With more child birth to American citizens, America's problems will be reduced and prosperity will improve for everyone. With more child birth to American citizens, we can save the soul of America.

Table of Contents

One

Whether you believe that Jesus Christ was the son of God or not, this story from Jesus gives us an important lesson. Jesus told a story about how talents were given to three servants to keep for their master. While those talents were presented in the story as money, those talents could have also been interpreted to be skills or knowledge or even the ability to reproduce. Well, when the master returned, he asked the servants to tell him what they did with the talents. Two of the servants made more talents from the talents that the master gave to them while the third servant did nothing with the talents. The master rewarded the first two servants by giving them even more talents. Then the master punished the third servant by taking the original talents away that were given to that servant and throwing that servant into the streets to suffer.

What does that story say to you?

To me, the moral of that story is that if people do more with the abilities (talents) that have been given to them, then they will receive more; but if people do not use their abilities (talents) to do more, to create more, to reproduce; then evolution or God or nature will take all of it away from those people and they will suffer. That is capitalism. That is survival of the fittest.

Prince of Peace, painted by Akiane, age 8. http://christianity. about.com/od/newtestamentpeople/p/jesuschrist.htm

It is obvious that more is given to those who do more, more is given to those who achieve more, more is given to those who have more. God, evolution, or nature rewards those who do more with their talents and penalizes those who do not. The meek might be blessed, but the strong survive and thrive. That is the truism of evolution. Those who do the most with their talents survive and thrive.

And if we as people are not using these talents that were provided to us by God or evolution or nature, then the future will be taken from us by God, evolution, or nature and we will suffer in the streets of death. And one of those talents is to reproduce.

Males and females are different from each other. Males and females have different body parts. Men and women are different from each other for a reason.

What is that reason?

People are born; they reproduce and then die.

BORN, REPRODUCE, DIE

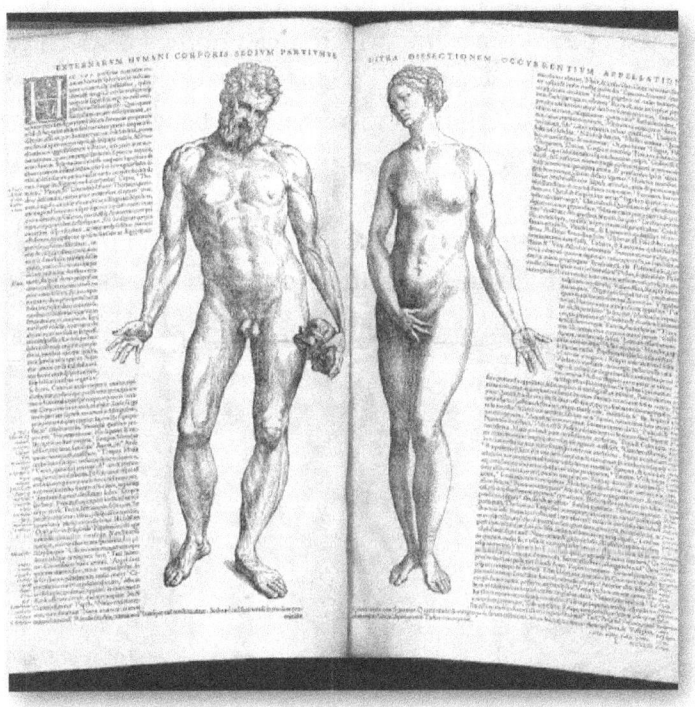

http://en.wikipedia.org/wiki/File:Externarvm_hvmani_
corporis_sedivm_partivmve,_1543..JPG

Whether Nature or God or evolution made women and men different from each other, the fact is that men are attracted to women, and women are attracted to men so that men and women will want to have sex with each other. It is natural. It is normal. Sex between a man and a woman is natural. Their body parts are made so a man's penis fits into a woman's vagina. There is no other reason for a man's penis to stand up or for a woman to have a vagina except for the act of sex together so they can make babies. That is normal. Any other sex is abnormal.

When the penis of the man is inside of the vagina of the woman, sperm from the man joins with an egg that is already inside of the woman. Magic happens. The sperm comes from the testicles of the man. The egg comes from the ovaries in the woman. The magic is that when the sperm from the man joins with the egg from the woman, a baby is created. No other types of sex can do this.

The unborn baby is small at first without looking much like a person. But it soon grows inside the woman and looks like a person within a couple of weeks. The woman has a child growing in her.

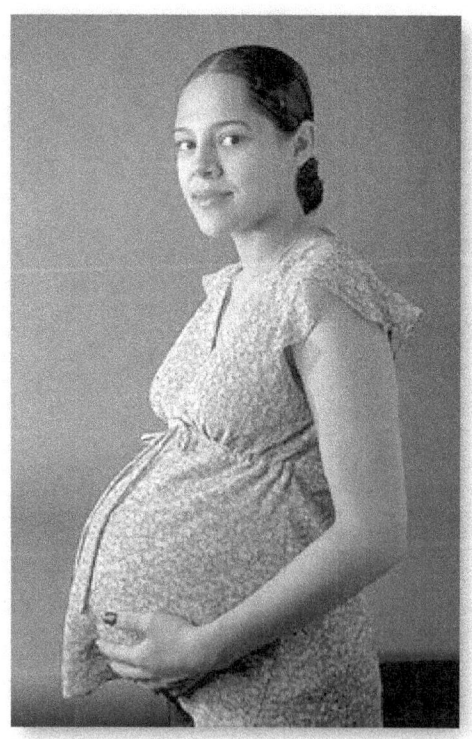

http://en.wikipedia.org/wiki/Pregnancy

The Birth Famine

After the egg in the woman is fertilized by the sperm from the man, the woman is now a mother who is carrying a small unborn child inside of her. The woman is nurturing the child inside of her as a mother. That child inside the mother has different blood than the mother. It has different characteristics than the mother. The child's own heart starts beating in the first 22 days. The DNA in the baby is different than the DNA in the mother. The baby in the mother is a different person from the mother.

The baby is attached to the mother by a cord inside of the mother where food travels from the mother to feed the baby. That cord is what the mother uses to nurture the unborn child. The baby is not part of the mother's body. The cord attaches them to each other. The baby grows inside the mother for about 9 months until it is ready to come out into the world.

The belly button is where each of us was attached to our mothers with the cord.

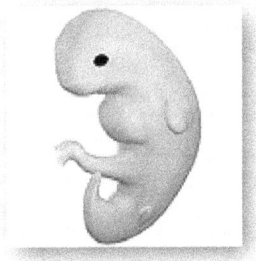

Embryo at 4 weeks after fertilization[16]

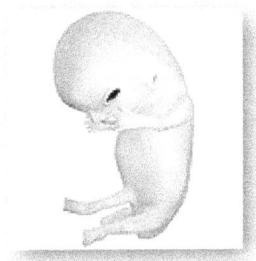

Fetus at 8 weeks after fertilization[17]

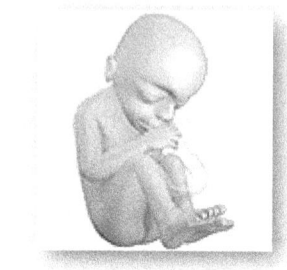

Fetus at 18 weeks after fertilization[18]

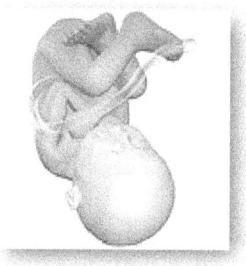

Fetus at 38 weeks after fertilization[19]
http://en.wikipedia.org/wiki/Pregnancy

There are other differences of a man to a woman. Like people, female lions are different from male lions as the result of evolution or nature or God as part of how the strongest of life survive.

http://en.wikipedia.org/wiki/Lion

The ovaries inside of a woman produce chemicals that are important to being a woman. Those chemicals are different than the ones in a man. The testicles in a man produce chemicals inside the man that are important to being a man. The chemicals in a man or woman are called hormones. The hormones in men are different than the hormones in women. All of this evolved as the strongest of any species survive.

The average woman is smaller than the average man. The average woman has more fat than the average man. The average woman has wider hips than the average man. A woman sheds blood from her uterus monthly when she is not fertilized by a man. A woman has breasts for feeding children that a man does not have.

The average man is larger than the average woman. The average man has more muscle than the average woman. The average man is built to perform better athletically than a woman. The hormones in a man make him more aggressive than a woman.

These differences between men and women allow women to be better at giving birth and caring for children while they allow men to be better at protecting and providing for their families. That is how God or Nature or evolution created men and women so they can survive and reproduce as a team of a man and a woman.

http://en.wikipedia.org/wiki/File:Pierre-Auguste_Renoir_146.jpg

This is the natural state of life. Women and men provide different functions for their families because they are biologically different. Both a man and woman are needed to create a baby. And Nature or God or evolution made is so men and women are attracted to each other so they want to have sex ... and that sex creates babies so that people reproduce.

Otherwise, God or Nature or evolution would not have made men and women be as different as they are from each other ... and not be sexually attractive to each other. Sex is how the strongest reproduce and survive. Reproduction is one of those important talents from God, or from Nature, or from evolution so that life reproduces itself. And to deny this important fact of how life perpetuates itself is to deny the truth. Men are different from women so they have sex to reproduce and replace themselves as they age and die.

Two

Why do we need babies?

When was the last time that you held a puppy or a kitten in your arms? How did it make you feel?

http://en.wikipedia.org/wiki/File:Polish_Tatra_Sheepdog_puppy.jpg

When was the last time that you held a baby in your arms? How did it make you feel?

http://en.wikipedia.org/wiki/File:Firmin_Baes_-_Doux_r%C3%AAves.jpg

So why is it that babies make us feel so good?

Could it be that a baby lets us know that life is going to continue? Is it that babies are so helpless that they make us feel needed? Could it be that we see a purpose for what we do each day when we see a baby? Could it be that babies are new, cute, and cuddly? Could it be that babies are innocent, without the problems that we carry with us each day?

We need to have children so we use our talents that were given to us or else we will lose those talents.

Babies feel good in our arms because they are good. They are innocent. They have not lived long enough to do anything wrong. They remind us about what it means to be good.

Babies are the beginning of life. In the spring, the new plants come up out of the ground. And in the fall, those plants turn brown and golden colors as they die. Babies are like the spring. They are the beginning of life. And without the spring, there will be no summer, no fall, and no winter.

We need babies so that life continues. We need babies so that we have spring in our lives. We need babies so that as each of us approaches the fall and winter of our own lives, we know that we added a bit more life and spring to the world by the babies that we gave to it. We need babies so that we know that we used our talents for good.

Aleta St. James was interviewed at 66 years old which was carried on Huffington Post on February 17, 2014. She gave birth to twins when she was 57 years old. When asked why she had children even though she was at an age that seemed too old to have children, she said that "children keep you young … and keep you on point."

So what do you think she meant when she said that children "keep you young … and keep you on point?"

Now use your abilities to figure things out and to determine what is right and what is wrong. If having children keeps a person on point, then what do you think is the point that she is discussing?

The point is this: Babies give meaning to our lives. Babies cannot live without the help of their parents. Babies need us. Babies make us feel needed. Babies are the real purpose for our own lives. We are here to help bring more life into the world. That is a talent that was given to us by Nature, by evolution, and by God. To not have children is a waste of that talent.

http://en.wikipedia.org/wiki/File:Baby_Robins_Ready_to_Feed.jpg
http://en.wikipedia.org/wiki/File:Baby_Robins_Ready_to_Feed.jpg

Couples who have children, have a totally different set of priorities than those who do not have any children. Parents learn to be selfless. Parents understand things at a subtle level about life that childless adults do not.

So which came first ... different priorities in life or children? Did having children change the priorities? Or is it that those who have life oriented priories before having children are the ones who have children?

Three

WHAT HAPPENS IF THERE ARE NOT ENOUGH CHILDREN?

F armers understand the importance of youth on a farm.

http://en.wikipedia.org/wiki/File:Ontario_farm.jpg

Female cows have udders to feed milk to their young. That milk is also consumed by humans.

http://en.wikipedia.org/wiki/File:Cow_female_black_white.jpg

According to a dairyman who was a customer of mine many years ago in Arizona, cows usually produce the most milk between 3 years old and 9 years old, and then typically die around 12 years old.

So let's say that we have 5 cows. One is 2 years old, one is 4 years old, one is 6 years old, one is 8 years old, and one is 10 years old. So what is the average age of our cows?

The average age is 6 years old. Well, according to that dairyman in Arizona, 6 years old would be about the average of the most productive cows. The 2 year old is probably not producing much milk and the 10 year old is probably not producing much either. So the middle 3 cows are actually producing the milk for our farm.

Let's pretend that it is 5 years from now. The cows die at 12 years old. Without any additional cows, in 5 years, 3 cows at ages of 7, 9, and 11 would still remain. The average age would be 9 years old.

So without getting any baby cows, the average age of the cows increased from 6 years old to 9 years old and the number of them decreased from 5 to 3. And probably only one of those cows can produce milk any longer, rather than 3 cows.

So what do you think is going to happen to the farm if it doesn't get some baby cows soon?

The average age of the cows will continue to get older. Eventually, no cows will be producing milk. There won't be any more milk to drink or to sell.

As the cows get older, they will need lots of care from veterinarians because older cows get sick more often than younger cows, but there won't be any milk to sell to pay the medical bills … so the last cows will die. The farm economy will suffer. Eventually, there won't be any cows. The farm will die and there won't be any milk to drink. The farm will become extinct.

http://en.wikipedia.org/wiki/File:Ainhoa_Croix1.JPG

What happened to the farm is also true about people. If we don't have enough children, then the average age of the people increases and the number of people decreases as people get older and die and there are not enough children to replace them.

Just like with the cows, older people need more help from doctors because they get sick more often than younger people. And older people don't produce as much products as they did when they were younger so there isn't as much money to pay those doctors.

The Roman Empire existed before, during, and after the time that Jesus Christ was alive on earth. Rome was the strongest of any empire. It stretched across most of the civilized world for more than five hundred years. It included what would be recognized today as most of Europe, most of the Middle East, and most of Northern Africa.

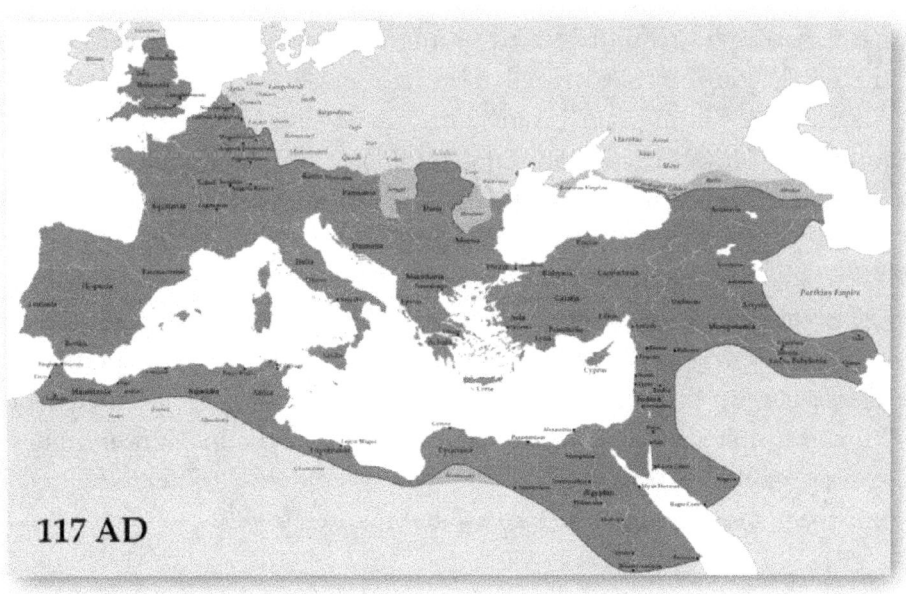

http://en.wikipedia.org/wiki/File:Roman_Empire_Trajan_117AD.png

Then something happened a couple of hundred years after Christ. The Romans did not give birth to enough children to maintain control of their empire. Homosexuality was common, multiple divorces per person were common, childless homes were common as too few Roman babies were made. Romans suffered from a birth famine.

The average age of Romans increased. As the average age of Romans increased because of not enough children being born, the Romans did not have enough young people to do the work. So the Romans allowed immigrants from outside of their empire to enter it to help take care of them, their homes, their vineyards, and their businesses. As the Romans aged, they needed a lot more health care and they relied on the immigrants to take care of them instead of having their own children take care of them.

The Romans could not even muster up enough young people to have an army to stop unwanted immigrants from invading them from the north. So the Romans relied on immigrants to protect them from the unwanted immigrant invaders instead of having their own children join the military. Those immigrants did not have the same loyalty to Rome and soon joined with the invading immigrant forces against the Romans.

Eventually, the immigrants outnumbered the Romans and the immigrants took over the Roman Empire ... slowly over a couple of generations. They cut it up into small city-sized countries and states. The size of the Roman Empire declined tremendously. The art, the magnificent cities, and the intellectual advances of the Romans crumbled. The Roman culture died. The Roman influence on the world ended.

Today, the only part left of the Roman Empire is Italy. It is the small boot shaped country in the middle of the map. That is it. That is all that remains of the Roman Empire.

The Birth Famine

Location of **Italy** (dark green) http://en.wikipedia.org/wiki/Italy

That is exactly what is happening in parts of the world today. The western world is suffering from a birth famine. Those counties that have low birth rates also have problems with their economies. The average ages of their citizens are increasing. They have fewer and fewer younger people to become soldiers. They have fewer and fewer younger people buying houses, cars, and other large products. The average costs per person for healthcare is increasing. Taxes on the younger people are increasing as there are fewer of them as a percent of the total population. And the excitement that comes from youth in a society is gone.

Greece, Germany, France, Spain, England, Scandinavia, Italy, Russia, the USA, Japan. What do they all have in common? They all are suffering from low birth rates of their own citizens.

And what are they doing to fix it?

Many of these countries are now allowing large amounts of immigrants into them so they have more young people to do the work, more young people to take care of the older people, more young people to become soldiers, more young people to buy houses and other large products, and more young people to pay taxes and healthcare insurance to support the older people.

But just like it was in the Roman Empire many years ago, allowing more immigrants is not working today. Immigrants do not just want to work in these countries; they want a bigger share of the money and a bigger share in running the governments. These immigrants come from the Middle East, South America, Africa, and Asia where the women give birth to lots of babies. Soon, the immigrants and their immediate offspring will outnumber the citizens of the countries that are allowing them to come in such large numbers.

Ryan Lovelace wrote a piece for "The Corner" on September 16, 2014 that was titled "Congressional Report: Foreign-Born Population Could Rise to 60 Million People within Ten Years." He states that "If the Senate's 2013 Gang of Eight immigration bill is implemented, the CRS report explains, the total foreign-born population could include nearly 68.3 million people by 2022." He continues with "one immigrant legally enters the U.S. every 40 seconds, according to U.S. Census Bureau data. The CRS report does not appear to consider the latest massive influx of Central Americans in its calculations, which suggests the number of foreign-born persons entering the U.S. in the next decade could be even greater than expected."

Let's discuss a couple of items from Ryan Lovelace's assessment. First, the Gang of Eight is a bi-partisan group in the Senate made up of 4 Democrats and 4 Republicans. Their united approach to immigration reform demonstrates that both parties want to increase the number of immigrants into the USA. Neither party is concerned about over-population in the USA. Both parties are more interested in increasing the USA population. Without immigration, the population of the USA would actually decrease since the birth rate of American citizens is so low. So all of these politicians want to increase immigration to increase the USA population.

Next, immigrants typically have more than 3 children per each woman. So as those immigrants have children born in the USA, the total of immigrants and their immediate offspring who are born in the USA will outnumber the number of the rest of Americans within 20 years.

And last, legal immigration has a much greater volume of immigration than does illegal immigration. "One immigrant legally enters the U.S. every 40 seconds." The government is playing a shell game with Americans. They have us focused on illegal immigration while they continue to increase legal immigration. Both legal immigration and illegal immigration are problems for working Americans.

An illegal shell game in Drottninggatan, a street in Stockholm.
http://en.wikipedia.org/wiki/Shell_game

In a shell game, "The operator's trick is sleight of hand. A skilled operator can remove a pea from under any shell (or shells) and place it under any shell (or shells), or keep it in his hand or up his sleeve, undetected by a mark. So it is never of any benefit for the mark to watch the movement of either the shells or the operator's hands; the pea will likely not be under any of the shells. When the operator has finished moving the shells around, he asks the mark if he wishes to bet on the play. If the mark agrees, he must set his money down before pointing to a shell. Using sleight of hand, the operator reveals the pea to be under a shell different from that chosen by the mark."

Yes, politicians are playing a shell game against Americans as the marks. Politicians are the operators of the shell game. We the people are their marks. They keep us focused on illegal immigrants while they allow massive amounts of legal immigrants. While the USA always allowed some immigrants into it, the USA never before now allowed the huge number of immigrants (legal or illegal) that are coming into the USA today. The government is deliberately allowing it. Republicans want more consumers and low paid employees for economic reasons while Democrats want more voters who will potentially vote for liberal socialists.

Each child born in the USA to an immigrant is automatically an American citizen with full voting privileges and becomes an "anchor baby" for its parents. Immigrants are motivated to have children in the USA quickly to "anchor" them in America.

Politicians are pandering to their constituencies. Republicans pander to businessmen and Democrats pander to socialists and feminists. No politicians are proposing legislation to encourage more child birth from American citizens. All of them are sacrificing the future of America for immediate political gains.

And the immigrants were never in such large amounts from countries that are so different from the people who already live in the USA. The prior immigrants were from places like Ireland and Germany and Italy where the laws and people and religions were like the ones of the people who were already living in the USA. The current immigrants are from Central America, South America, Asia, the Middle East, and Africa.

The Birth Famine

When the new immigrants and their immediate offspring outnumber the citizens of any country, what do you think will happen to that country?

What will happen to its schools?

What will happen to the costs for services provided by government?

What will happen to healthcare costs?

What will happen to what is shown on TV and movies?

What will happen to its jobs?

What will happen to the pay for workers?

What will happen to the rules of the country?

What will happen to the culture?

Would it surprise anyone if immigrants want to separate the states with lots of them from the USA? Like California or Florida or Texas? Would it surprise you if those states want to secede from the USA some day?

The last chapters of this book present ideas of how to reform immigration to the USA. They are radical ideas that are needed to save America.

Four

How many children do we need?

Let's assume that the average American citizen lives about 80 years. Harry Dent discusses the stages of life in his book "The Demographic Cliff," published by the Penguin Group in 2014.

The first 20 years of life are much like the spring. A person is born and grows into an adult in those first 20 years. This is the growth and learning time. Most people go to school or learn a trade, make lots of friends, and learn how to take care of themselves.

Between the ages of 20 and 40, life is more like the summer. A person starts a career, starts purchasing products, gets married, and raises children. Income is increasing, debt is also increasing, and consumption is increasing a lot.

Between the ages of 40 and 60, life is rewarding. This is the beautiful time of autumn. Just like with autumn, all the crops of a person's life are ready for harvest. This is when people usually reach their highest job positions and the highest incomes. Their children are going to high school/college/trade schools, becoming adults, and leaving home. Consumption of things like houses, cars, furnishings, and other products is at its highest.

Income exceeds debt as it is finally possible for these people to keep some of their income as savings for older age.

People who are over 60 years old are in the winter of life. They can see that the end of life is not too far away. Most are retired with fixed incomes. Consumption of products is low while healthcare needs and costs are growing at a very fast pace. They buy lots of services from accountants and doctors with low economic multipliers rather than buying manufactured products like cars and new houses with high economic multipliers. They rely on their children to help them and they rely on younger people to pay taxes so the government can help them. So where are you on this chart?

before 20	**20 to 40**	**40 to 60**	**over 60**
springtime of life	summer of life	autumn of life	winter of life
learning/growing	starting career	career objectives achieved	retired
limited product consumption	increasing product consumption	highest product consumption	low product consumption. Mostly service consumption.
school/college/trade	getting married and starting families	children in high school, trade schools, and college	grandparents
healthy	raising children	children leaving home	high healthcare costs
little income	increasing income/debt	highest income/taxes	fixed income

So why is this important?

If there are not enough people between the ages of 40 and 60, then the government is not receiving enough taxes to help take care of the people who are over 60. If there are not enough people who are between 40 and 60, then the economy suffers because not enough products are being bought to keep younger people employed.

If there are not enough people between 20 and 40, then there are not enough people who are healthy to balance health insurance costs for those who are over 60 and then there will not be enough people between 40 and 60 when the current 40 to 60 year old people get older.

If there are not enough people who are under 20 years old, then there are not enough low paid workers and apprentice workers, and there will not be enough people between 20 and 40 when those current people between 20 and 40 get older.

Today, the USA has too high of a percent of "citizens" who are over 60 and too low of a percent of "citizens" who are younger. The government does not receive enough taxes from the younger citizens to help take care of these older people because those people who are over 60 did not have enough children when they were between 20 and 40.

A country that wants to sustain a balance in its population should have about a quarter of its "citizen" population under 20, a quarter between 20 and 40, a quarter between 40 and 60, and a quarter over 60. To do that, every man and woman needs to have enough children to replace each man and woman as they age and die. Therefore, each woman needs to have at least 2 children to replace her and a man.

To maintain a population, then each woman needs to have at least 2 children.

The Birth Famine

A balanced population is ¼ under 20, ¼ between 20 and 40, ¼ between 40 and 60, ¼ over 60.

If a country wants to grow its citizen population, then each citizen woman needs to have more than 2 children and the country needs to have more than a quarter of its population under 20 years old.

Think about this: if half of the citizen women have no children, then the other half must have 4 children per each one to have an average of 2 per each. According to the Congressional Research Report that was mentioned earlier in this book, more than half the young people today do not plan to have any children at all … not ever!

The only way that the USA is maintaining a balanced population is by allowing massive amounts of immigration because the citizens are not raising enough of their own children. And just like in the Roman Empire many years ago, that massive amount of immigration is causing massive problems for the country….lower wages for citizen workers, higher costs for government services, higher costs for healthcare per person, higher costs for education per student, and higher crime rates.

Five

My friend Father Tim said to me that as a society is more educated, it has fewer children because it values other things as more important than having children. He also said that as a society is more intelligent, it learns more ways to justify its bad actions (sins).

Scientists at Oxford University in England recently discovered a small piece of the brain that determines right from wrong. (http://www.theguardian.com/science/2014/jan/28/grass-greener-brain-research-lateral-frontal-pole) It is the conscience for a person. Some are larger for some people and some are smaller. Those scientists at Oxford might say that more intelligent people use their intelligence (logic) to fool that little part of the brain that understands right from wrong rather than accept natural moral standards. Pleasure overrides conscience by the use of educated logic… people use their intelligence to justify and rationalize sinful behavior … they use their intelligence to fool their consciences.

Let's use our talents to try to figure out why intelligent and wealthy people do not have as many children as those who are poorer and less educated …. especially since having enough children is so important for the survival of a country, of a group of people, or of a society. And then let's figure out what will happen next if it continues.

Children require work. They require care. They require attention. They require time.

http://en.wikipedia.org/wiki/File:Baby_Robins_Ready_to_Feed.jpg
http://en.wikipedia.org/wiki/File:Baby_Robins_Ready_to_Feed.jpg

Sometimes that care for children keeps parents from doing other things. It can keep them from being able to travel for work which can keep them from getting promoted and earning more money. It can keep them from being able to work late and earn more money. It can keep them from being able to go out with their friends. It can cost them more for help like baby sitting or day care which takes money away from vacations or buying new things like jewelry or furs.

So many adults today choose to not have children, or they choose to have too few children so they can have things and life styles that they want.

How many adults do you know who do not have any children, or maybe only one child? So how many children do other citizens need to raise to make up for those adults who have none or just one?

A good friend, Sue Sarkis sent an email to me on July 4, 2014 where she states that a big contributor to the low birth rate is the example set by role models of our younger people. She states:

> The younger generations do not have enough proper role models, are not being raised in a home with a family environment, and are more concerned about their own personal wants and desires. They have absolutely no desire to procreate because they are just down-right STUPID and selfish!!!

> Just this morning there was a segment on The Today Show about why Cameron Diaz, George Clooney, etc. are not having children. It was quite depressing. I'll insert past statements they have made below.....

> ... We were basically put here to procreate. Ask any animal. Cats, dogs, horses, elephants, giraffes, and all others have more darn brains than the homo sapiens in this day and age. Without pro-creation, we cannot survive. In the case of us white folks, we are killing off our own race. In the case of Jews, they are killing off their own heritage. The Asians are killing off their own culture.

> Here's just a few comments that have been made in recent times:

> Chelsea Handler has said, "I definitely don't want to have kids. I don't think I'd be a great mother. I don't want to have a kid and have it raised by a nanny. I don't have the time to raise a child myself."

The Birth Famine

John Hamm told US Weekly, "I'd be a terrible father! I see my friends who have children and I'm like, 'Dude, how are you even upright, much less here at work at 6 AM?'"

George Clooney has said, "I've always known fatherhood wasn't for me. Raising kids is a huge commitment and has to be your top priority. For me, that priority is my work. That's why I'll never get married again".

Ricky Gervais said, "We never wanted to be parents, with all that entails: the loss of freedom, total dependency, I'm the sort of person who has to check three times that I've shut the door, so I'd probably stare at a kid all day to check it was breathing."

Margaret Cho has said, "I don't have children, and I am not sure if I have wanted them or never wanted them. It's weird not to be able to decide. I don't know if I could stand that kind of commitment, or if I am really honest, I don't think that I could handle being that vulnerable to someone else."

Jay and Mavis Leno have said that they never planned on having children. "I had made up my mind when I was little that I would never get married or have children, so I had no agenda," Mavis told the LA Times in 2009.

Renee Zellweger has said she never had any desire to have children. She said, "I just want to be independent and be able to take care of myself."

When asked if she ever wanted to have children, comedian Janeane Garofalo said "I thought that I did. Now I realize that I don't."

Kim Catrall - "When I answered those questions regarding having children, I realized that so much of the pressure I was feeling was from outside sources, and I knew I wasn't ready to take that step into motherhood," Catrall wrote on Oprah.com about her realization she didn't want to have children. "Being a biological mother just isn't part of my experience this time around," she added. In her case since she changes boyfriends like men change socks, it's probably better off for any child.

Oprah Winfrey has stated that she has no desire to have a child.

Bottom Line: (these are) Egocentric role models!!!

https://www.google.com/?gws_rd=ssl#q=%22%22I+definitely+don't+want +to+have+kids.+I+don't+think+I'd+be+a+great+mother.+I+don't+want+to+ have+a+kid+and+have+it+raised+by+a+nanny.+I+don't+have+the+time+to+ raise+a+child+myself%22

https://www.google.com/?gws_rd=ssl#q=%22I'd+be+a+terrible+fa ther!++I+see+my+friends+who+have+children+and+I'm+like%2C +'Dude%2C+how+are+you+even+upright%2C+much+less+here+ at+work+at+6+AM%3F'%22

https://www.google.com/?gws_rd=ssl#q=%22+%22I've+always+known+fa therhood+wasn't+for+me.+Raising+kids+is+a+huge+commitment+and+has +to+be+your+top+priority.+For+me%2C+that+priority+is+my+work.%22

http://www.crushable.com/2013/12/26/entertainment/ celebrities-who-dont-want-kids-babies/2/

The Birth Famine

The more educated nations and wealthy nations have the fewest children per women. The most educated and wealthy people in the USA have the fewest children.

Did the educated and wealthy people stop having sex? No. Adults find too much pleasure in having sex, so those educated and wealthy people who do not want to have children learned how to enjoy sex without making babies.

Let me say this slowly. Adults have sex without making babies because they want the pleasure of sex without having to give up owning more things and doing more stuff. And they perceive that raising children will keep them from owning more things and doing more stuff.

There are 2 ways that these educated, wealthy adults keep from having children.

One way to not make a baby is to keep the sperm from fertilizing an egg.

But if the sperm should fertilize the egg, then the other way to keep from having to raise the child is to kill it.

We can minimize killing an unborn child by calling it something other than murder, but it is murder just the same. Educated people, intelligent people, use their education/intelligence to justify killing an unborn child as something other than murder ... that is logic to fool the conscience part of the brain ... but it is murder just the same since the unborn child is a different person from the mother.

There are many ways to keep the sperm from reaching the egg.

One way is to not allow the penis to enter the vagina. The man and the woman do other things to feel good sexually without actually allowing the penis to enter the vagina.

Some men have homosexual sex with other men and some women have homosexual sex with other women. Homosexuality is one of the reasons why the Roman Empire had too little child birth. Paul even wrote about it in the Bible in Romans 1:21.

Another way is for a man to wear a condom. It catches all the sperms in it which keeps them from fertilizing the egg.

A third way is for the woman to use chemicals in her vagina that kill the sperms. Those chemicals can harm the woman if they are used too often.

A forth way is for the woman to have a diaphragm implanted in her that stops the sperms from reaching the egg.

A fifth way is for the woman to take pills or wear patches that keep the eggs from being released from the ovaries. Then the sperm cannot reach the egg.

A sixth way is for either the man or the woman to have an operation that either keeps the sperm from leaving the man or keeps the egg from entering the uterus. Both of those methods keep the sperm from being able to fertilize the egg. Both of them are fairly permanent. This is a method of sterilization.

Some scientists have been developing methods to use chemicals to sterilize women and men. Some of those chemicals would keep the men from making live sperm. Other chemicals would kill all the eggs in a woman.

How hard would it be to put chemicals in food or water without us knowing about it?

All of these methods keep the sperm from fertilizing the egg. They are collectively called "birth control."

Birth Control	Who	How permanent?
non intercourse sex	both	not
homosexuality	both	not
condom	man	not
vagina chemicals	woman	can be dangerous
diaphragm	woman	not
pills or patches	woman	can have side effects
sterilization operation	both	very
sterilization drugs	both	very

Let's say that the sperm reaches the egg and fertilizes it. At that moment of conception, a child starts growing inside of the mother.

Since the child is a different person from the mother and that unborn baby is not part of the mother's body, then the only way for that newly conceived child to not be born is to kill it. Intelligent people try to define this murder as birth control, but it is still murder. Sometimes a child will die on his or her own, but not very often. So if the mother does not want the child to be born, then she must kill it.

Now, you might say that the father has a role in killing it also, but the Supreme Court of the United States disagrees with you. Our Supreme Court ruled in 1973 that it is a "woman's right to choose" the outcome of her child, and no one else's. Therefore, the child can only be killed by the mother. Therefore, many men feel no responsibly for the child.

Since 1973, the percent of children who are born without a father to help raise them has more than tripled. Since it is a "woman's right to choose," many men feel no responsibility for pregnancy. Legalizing abortion increased the number of children raised in fatherless homes.

How do you feel about this?

OK, so how does a mother kill an unborn child?

If the child has only just started growing within a couple of days, then the mother can take a pill which fools her body into passing the child out of it. That pill is called a morning-after pill. Passing the child out of her body kills the child.

If the child is more than a couple of days old, then the mother kills the child by having an abortion. An abortion is a procedure done by a doctor that kills and removes the baby from the mother. The doctor spreads the woman's legs and then inserts medical tools into the vagina of the woman which kills the child. Then the doctor removes the child from the mother by either pulling it out with tools or by using a machine that sucks it out. In either case, the child is destroyed and often pulled apart by its limbs and other body parts. Then the dead child is thrown away like any other medical garbage.

These are a few of the tools used by the doctor to perform an abortion:

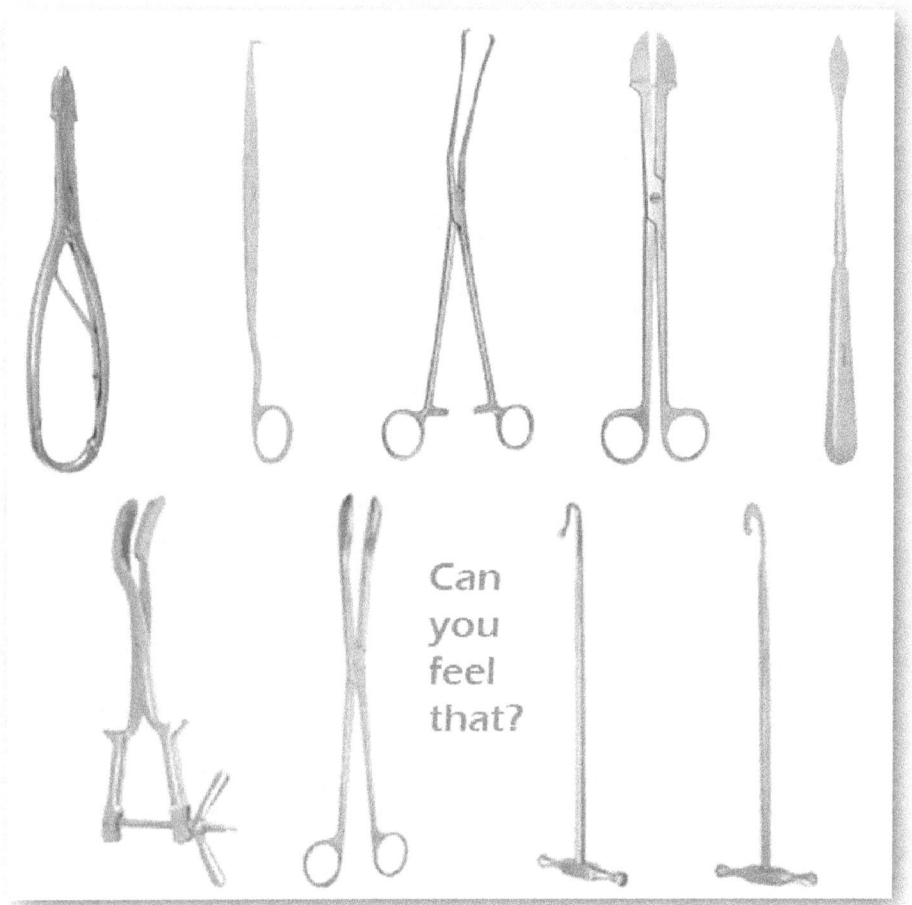

a collection of abortion instruments
http://clinicquotes.com/pictures-of-the-tools-used-to-perform-abortions/

When the child is close to being ready to be born, an abortion at that time is called a late term abortion. Sometimes the child actually breaths and lives when the doctor takes it out of the mother during a late term abortion. Rather than helping the child live, the doctor or nurse might let it die. They keep it from getting any water or food. They leave it alone on a table, cold, hungry, thirsty, and alone to die. The child starves to death. That is called infanticide.

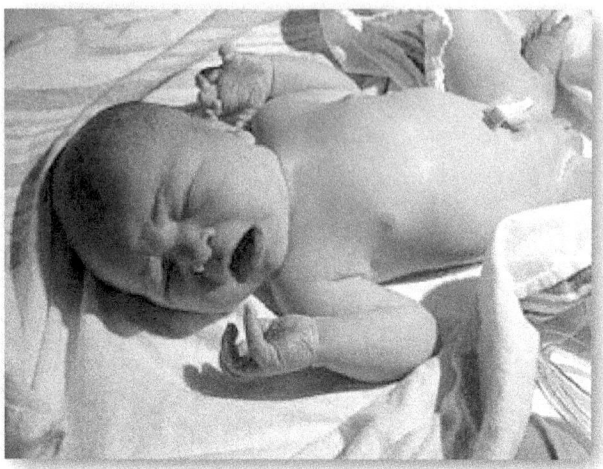

http://en.wikipedia.org/wiki/Childbirth

How do you feel about all of this? Is it OK with you? What if your mother had an abortion instead of allowing you to be born? Or what if she allowed you to die when you were born?

Even though the Supreme Court said that a mother has the legal right to choose to have an abortion, to you, are abortion and infanticide morally OK to do?

With all the methods available for birth control, why is there any need for abortions and infanticide? Because some people have no self control when it comes to having sex. They have sex without using birth control because they know that if the woman becomes pregnant, then she can get an abortion, so why worry about birth control?

Many people are concerned about peace in the world, but miss the big picture about abortion. There will be no trust between people to promote peace as long as there is legal abortion. Mother Theresa of Calcutta said this about peace (from Rules for Conservatives): "The greatest destroyer of peace is abortion ... many are dying deliberately by the will of the mother.

And this is what is the greatest destroyer of peace today. Because if a mother can kill her own child, what is left for me to kill you and you to kill me? There is nothing in between."

So what happens next? Why are we having so few children? Why is the western world in a birth famine?

Well, the future is in each of our hands. Will it be a good future or a future like the one that faced the Roman Empire?

Children are the supreme blessing from God, from nature, and from evolution. So may we all be blessed with many happy and healthy children. May we have a future.

Because if there are no children, then there is no future.

But if there are enough children, then the future is bright like the morning sun in the spring.

http://en.wikipedia.org/wiki/File:Sun_rise_at_CuaLo.jpg

Six

At the end of the record album "Abby Road," the Beatles sang:

"And in the end, the love you take is equal to the love you make."

Children are a product of love. So what does it say about a society that does not want to make enough children?

What can we do about it? In the end, the answer to this question will make all the difference.

This chapter is for those who want to fix the low birth rate problem of American citizens.

Jesus said that A. anyone who rejects a little one (child) also B. rejects him.

Jesus also said that anyone who B. rejects him will be C. rejected by him to his father in heaven.

If A = B and B = C, then A = C. Therefore, rejection of children = rejection by Jesus to God, his father.

So why would so many people risk being rejected by Jesus because they rejected him by not having children? Why would they risk being rejected by Jesus by having abortions?

Many Americans reject Jesus in the form of children so they can own lots more things and do lots more things. Things and life styles and careers are more important to them than children. Things and life styles and careers are more important to them than rejection by Jesus. Short term pleasure is more important than eternal damnation. Book smart and life stupid.

The birth rate for white people is so low at this time that the population of whites will decrease by half within the next 50 years. The white population of the world has decreased from 24% of the world population to less than 10% in just the last 50 years. That is truly a birth famine.

Even more striking is the birth rate for Jewish people. National Socialists (Nazis) killed 6 million Jews of the 17 million Jews who were alive in the world in 1938 in the WWII Holocaust along with 6 million Catholics and gypsies. In the 65 years since the end of WWII in 1945, the population of Jewish people in the world only increased by 20% (2 million additional Jews) to 13 million while Catholics increased by 500% in the same time period. In the 65 years since the end of WWII, Jews did not reproduce enough to even replace those 6 million Jews who died in the Holocaust. At a birth rate of just 2.5 children per woman, the Jewish population would be more than 60 million after the 3 generations since 1945 instead of 13 million. That would have been the same 500% increase as to Catholics. 13 million Jews is less than 2/10^{ths} of one percent of the world population. At the current birth rate for Jews, the Jewish population in the world could be less than 5 million within 50 years. Of all the famines that inflicted Jews in their 5,000 year history, this famine could be the worst. Jews have a birth rate for extinction.

The Birth Famine

Wouldn't you think that bringing life into the world is more important to God and Nature and evolution than anything else? Wouldn't you think that raising children is most important?

So what does it say to you about those groups of people who do not want to have children?

Yes, many people spout rhetoric about helping the poor or saving baby whales or helping people in undeveloped countries or saving the environment, but when asked to sacrifice something of their own lives to raise children, they bolt. They are hypocrites. They say great things, but lack the sincerity to sacrifice anything from their own lives to even raise their own children.

Many people hide behind the misconception that they are helping solve a world population problem by not having children. That is just the use of rationalization that Father Tim discussed. The USA is allowing massive amounts of immigrants to offset its low birth rate, so it is obvious that the USA leaders want the population to increase ... not decrease. Europe allows massive amounts of immigrants to offset its low birth rate. So it is obvious that European leaders want its population to increase ... not decrease. Japan is losing population and suffers economically because of its low birth rate. The governments of the USA and Western Europe understand that the low birth rates are hurting them, but those governments refuse to step up to fixing the real problem. Instead, they encourage massive immigration to offset their low birth rates which causes huge problems on a per capita basis of increased government costs, increased crime, increased healthcare needs, increased education needs, and deterioration to western values.

If only small amounts of immigrants entered the receiving countries, then those immigrants would easily assimilate into their host countries.

Large amounts do not assimilate. Governments in the western world are allowing large amounts of immigration to destroy their cultures just because they will not step up and solve the root causes of low birth rates to their citizens.

The world outside of Europe, Japan, and the USA adds 80 million new people each year. The 4 or 5 million who immigrate to Europe and the USA each year do nothing to help the overpopulation caused by those 80 million additional people in the rest of the world each year. But massive immigration does extreme harm to the receiving countries. Caucasians use the world population to justify their own short sighted selfishness for things and money and careers and life styles. And in the end, this birth famine will cost dearly.

This is about karma. It is about reaping where you sow. It is about "going forth and multiplying." It is about adhering to the rules of nature and evolution and God. Take your pick as to which one. God, Nature, and evolution all reward reproduction and punish those nations, societies, and races that do not reproduce just as Jesus said would happen to those who waste their talents.

A society that has too few children is an aging society. As the average age increases, so do its average medical costs per person. As the average age increases, then the consumption of hard products decreases and the economy suffers. As the average age increases and more people retire than join the work force, then the taxes increase per working person ... especially Social Security taxes. As the average age increases, then the burden on the younger people to care for the older people increases per each younger person.

Many politicians will claim that the USA average age is stable. They will claim that the average age of Americans is not increasing. They lie.

The Birth Famine

The average age of American "citizens" is increasing. If the average age of all people in the USA is stable, that is only because of the massive numbers of immigrants who keep the total average age lower than what it is for citizens. This is about all immigrants, not just Mexican immigrants. The USA receives legal immigrants from Africa, Asia, and South America in huge numbers … not just illegal immigrants from Mexico. The average age of American citizens is increasing. Those massive amounts of immigrants cause other horrible problems. And those immigrants do nothing to help off-load the economic and psychological burdens placed on the younger American citizens from an aging population. The burden to care for 2 parents is much greater for an only-child than it is for 3 or 4 siblings.

This next chart shows how the bubble of Baby Boomers affected the overall population for the last 40 years. It is from Flatrock on the internet about "population pyramids." Notice how the Baby Boom bubble moves higher on the graph from 1970 to 1990 to and then to 2010. And then notice how the average age of Americans increased as the Baby Boom bubble advanced in age. It should be noted that the economy of the USA boomed in the 1990s as Baby Boomers were in their 40s. And the economy suffered in 2010 as Baby Boomers grew older than 60. It should also be noted that the pyramid is only smoothing out from the Baby Boom bubble of 1970 as more and more young immigrants are admitted into the USA. Without immigration, the average age would increase much more. If Baby Boomers had just had 2 children per each woman, the bubble would have naturally disappeared in 1990 and 2010 and the average age of Americans would not have increased … and that is affecting everything today.

1970	1990	2010
POPULATION: 203.2 million	POPULATION: 248.7 million	POPULATION: 282.6 million
MEDIAN AGE: 27.9	MEDIAN AGE: 32.9	MEDIAN AGE: 39

As you look at the next chart, please notice that it is from 1993. For several decades, at least since 1993, our leaders have been aware of the problem of increased immigration to augment the low birth rate. As discussed in my previous books, several congressmen told me that they were well aware of the low birth rate by 1990 and the problems it was causing to America, yet they did nothing to correct the root causes to a low birth rate for American citizens. Instead, they allowed massive immigration to try to compensate for the low birth rate.

This next chart is from http://www.susps.org/overview/numbers.html

"The top line of the following graph shows actual U.S. population from 1970 to 1993, and the U.S. Census Bureau "medium projection" of total population size from 1994 to 2050.[2] It assumes fertility, mortality, and mass immigration levels will remain similar to 1993. In fact, overall immigration has continued to rise significantly, meaning that population growth will actually be higher than shown below.[31]"

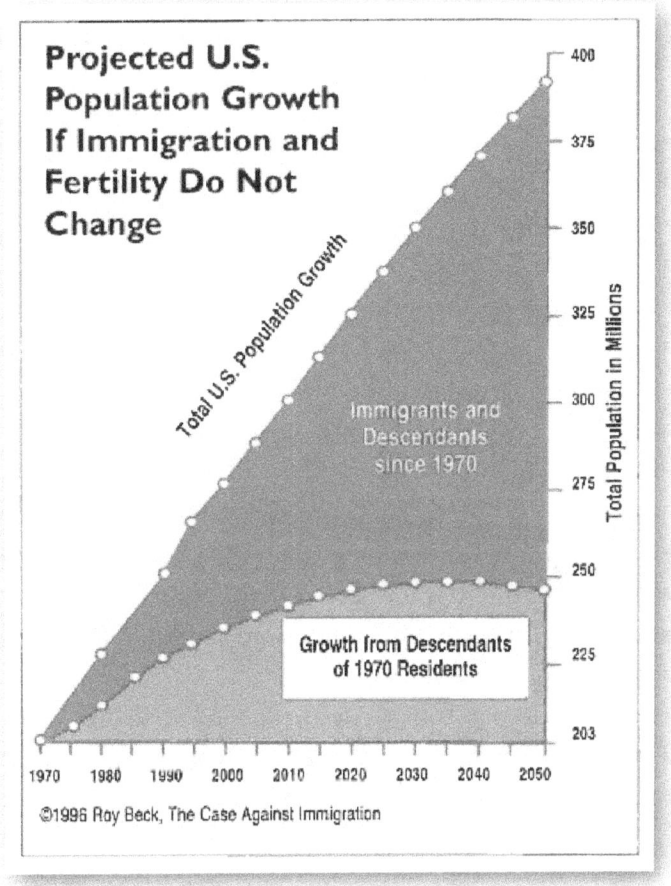

Projected U.S. Population Growth If Immigration and Fertility Do Not Change

Total U.S. Population Growth

Immigrants and Descendants since 1970

Growth from Descendants of 1970 Residents

Total Population in Millions

400
375
350
325
300
275
250
225
203

1970 1980 1990 2000 2010 2020 2030 2040 2050

©1996 Roy Beck, The Case Against Immigration

Sources: U.S. Census Bureau; demographer Leon Bouvier[11]

Roy Beck, Numbers USA

As can be seen, all growth to the USA population is from immigration and the offspring of those immigrants. The immigrant portion of the USA population will have grown from almost nothing in 1970 to more than 40% of the total by 2050 and that does not include their offspring. According to the Congressional Research Group, immigrants and their immediate offspring who are born in the USA will outnumber the rest of Americans in the USA within the next 20 years.

Immigration is the only thing that keeps the average age of people in the USA from rising even faster. Without massive immigration, the population of the USA would actually decrease and the average age would increase dramatically because of the low birth rate to citizens ... especially as we Baby Boomers exceed 60 years old without having produced enough children to replace ourselves as we moved out of the 40 to 60 year old bracket.

Dr. James Lange belongs to an internet discussion group along with me. We rarely agree on issues. On immigration, we found some common ground. He posted this comment from his email address of langej@msn.com on July 28, 2014:

> **Illegal immigrants** also show the desirable adventuresome and entrepreneurial spirit, but they have two disadvantages: they may not have skills that are needed in our economy and they are scoff-laws.
>
> If they do not have the skills we need, they end up in minimum-wage jobs that are already over-crowded and hence keep the wages for these jobs at the bottom of the natural range. This effect is exacerbated by the illegal immigrants' need to stay hidden from the law, which means they cannot complain about either wages or working conditions. As a result, the bottom tier of our native born citizens, who we have failed to educate, must compete for jobs that do not pay enough to feed, clothe and house their children, thus forcing them onto welfare hand-outs to survive. This, in turn, creates a culture of dependency and a significant section of the electorate with a vested interest in increasing either wages or hand-outs.
>
> The effect on our society of being a scoff-law is perhaps even worse. Not only do the illegal immigrants learn from experience that it is foolish to obey any inconvenient law of their adopted country, their children - seeing visible evidence that obeying inconvenient laws is not necessary – become scoff-laws as well. Even if subsequently

regularised & naturalised, illegal immigrants and their offspring make poorer citizens and weaken the social contract.

As per Dr. Lange, illegal immigration "creates a culture of dependency and a significant section of the electorate with a vested interest in increasing either wages or hand-outs."

So why do politicians continue to use immigration to increase the population instead of solving the root cause to the birth rate for American citizens? Why do they allow America to follow in the footsteps of Western Europe and of the ancient Roman Empire? They do it:

1. Because their lust for power is more important to them than solving this problem. And that lust for power keeps them from taking actions that are politically incorrect with liberals, feminists, and gays.
2. Because some politicians want to increase the portion of society who are dependent on government to increase the voters who are dependent on keeping them in office.
3. Because Americans have learned to outsource/subcontract anything and everything. Immigration is just a method of outsourcing child birth to achieve population growth.

Like me, Mike Towers has been trying to get people to realize the problems with using immigration to augment our low birth rate. He wrote the following piece in 2010.

May 30, 2010 An untold story about illegal immigration

The usual arguments surrounding illegal immigration seem to have polarized into two general categories:

The argument typified by the political right, states this is simply a crime that must absolutely be stopped, and in fact, reversed by sending these illegal immigrants home as soon as possible.

From the left, you will usually hear the vast majority of these folks are simply coming from horrible poverty to take jobs that most Americans won't do.

I was caught between these two arguments for many years. I couldn't support the notion that anyone could enter our country illegally and be allowed to stay. However, I could also understand why anyone with no other way to earn enough money to support their family would take the risk.

My personal views changed a few years ago when I met a gentleman while golfing in the Palm Springs area of California. I went to a resort golf course alone and was paired up with three strangers. The fellow I shared a golf cart with was in his early 70s and appeared to be highly educated and was very well spoken. It turned out he was a rather prominent economist who had been a career professor at an Ivy League school, and had been a member of the White House Council of Economic Advisers for Presidents Bill Clinton and George H. W. Bush.

For some reason -- I don't remember why -- the topic of illegal immigration came up. This fellow asked me what I thought about the issue. I immediately launched into arguments against it. I complained about jobs being taken from Americans, the fact many of these folks were paid under the table and thus both they and their employers were avoiding taxes. I added my concerns about the huge public expense being absorbed by the rest of us for education and health care for these illegal immigrants and their children.

This gentleman told me I needed a serious amount of education on the topic. So I invited him to educate me. I fully expected the typical liberal rhetoric about the need for empathy and humanity, but instead, he asked me an interesting question: "Do you really believe if the United States government, with the most powerful military in the world, really didn't want these folks coming in that we couldn't stop them?" He added that Canada didn't have any problems doing so.

He went on to tell me he had been involved in many discussions with some of the top leaders in our country from both major political parties for the past three decades, during which a policy of allowing these immigrants to enter illegally was openly and broadly supported.

I was quite surprised and frankly more than a little disbelieving. I asked him why our leaders would do such a thing ....

... He said the birthrate in the United States had been so low over the past few decades we will not have enough young workers coming of age in the future to provide sufficient tax revenues to fund the entitlements needed by the 77 million baby boomers set to begin reaching retirement age in 2011.

He also said no civilization with a long-term birthrate below 2 per female had ever survived. The United States has been hovering in the 1.7 to 1.8 rate for decades. He said that our leaders knew what was coming and had elected to allow the illegal immigration because it was the least expensive and most expedient solution.

He said almost every developed nation was in the exact same situation and most were taking similar steps, though most had legalized immigration through guest-worker programs. He also mentioned that the country in the most trouble in terms of sustainability was Japan because its birthrate was even below ours and they will allow almost no immigration.

He went on to say we should be focused on making sure these illegal immigrants become citizens as soon as possible (thus maximizing tax revenues), and make sure our own children and those of the illegal immigrants get the best education possible in order to improve their overall earning capacity -- and the taxes collected. He also said we were fortunate because most of our illegal immigrants are Hispanic and are generally Christians with a deep love of family.

I asked him why our leaders haven't just leveled with the American people if this is all true? He said it's sad, but our leaders think the average American citizen isn't smart enough to understand .....

Mike Tower
miketower@bellsouth.net

That statistic of 1.7 births per woman is for all women ... including immigrants. The average birth rate for American citizen women is much lower, especially for Caucasian women ... which is currently less than one per woman.

Many more immigrants enter the USA legally than illegally. Legal immigration is more of a problem than is illegal immigration.

Just as in business, child birth vs. more immigration is a "make or buy" decision. As in business, this is a decision to either grow internally or from external means. And in business, there are advantages to making a product component vs. buying that component. There are advantages to internal growth vs. external growth. The same is true about child birth. A business considers several factors when deciding to make its own components or to buy those components from subcontractors. Those factors can include:

MAKE	**or BUY (outsource)**
Quality control	Lower risk
Lower long term costs	Lower start up costs
Brand integrity	Lower commitment
Patent protection	Lower investment

The Birth Famine

Typically, a business will outsource the manufacturing of a component when it is for the short term and the business cannot afford to manufacture the component itself. Otherwise, the long term impact from subcontracting manufacturing to outsourcers will eventually cause quality problems, increased costs, brand deterioration, and patent infringements. A business will try to grow internally ... promote from within its ranks ... to preserve its culture; and it will choose to grow by external means only when competition and market conditions demand external growth.

Americans are outsourcing the birth and growth of the American population rather than do the job internally. The problems of that are the same as when businesses outsource their activities to others. That will eventually cause quality problems, increased costs, brand deterioration, and patent infringements. Growth from external means will ultimately destroy the culture.

When our own government chooses to allow more immigration rather than do what is necessary to encourage more child birth, it is choosing to have a lower commitment and investment in our nation rather than lower our long term costs and protect the culture of America. It is choosing the path of least immediate political costs/resistance. Eventually, that will lead to brand deterioration, to greater long term costs, and to the deterioration of quality control of American values. That will provide the smallest return on investment in the long term. A continual long term "buy" decision (immigration) will produce a long term loss economically and culturally.

In the end, history will record that the years between 1985 and 2005 boomed economically in Europe and the USA because Baby Boomers were in those magic years of product consumption and income performance that happen naturally between 40 and 60 years old. Baby Boomers who were born between 1945 and 1960 helped the economy when they were between 40 and 60 years old. The economy boomed. Governments, Clinton and W. Bush, had nothing to do with the economic boom. It was all about demographics.

But as Baby Boomers entered that stage above 60 years old, the effect of the lack of births by Baby Boomers has been devastating. Between 40 and 60 years old, Baby Boomers traveled all over the world, bought huge houses, drove luxury cars, got divorced (several times for some), committed adultery, smoked pot, used lots of other drugs, played, played, and played some more, and did what ever felt good. Baby Boomers made the economies of the western world smoking hot. But Baby Boomers did not even produce enough children to replace themselves. So as Baby Boomers left those economically important years of 40 to 60, the economy suffered because there were not enough citizens between 20 and 40 to move into the 40 to 60 bracket to replace the Baby Boomers.

Eventually, the morals of a society impact the economy of that society. The low birth rate and/or massive immigration to augment the low birth rate are direct results of a deteriorating set of morals. They are dramatically affecting the economies of the USA, Western Europe, and Japan right now. A birth rate that does not at least replace each man and each woman (at least 2 children per woman) is way too low. It is against nature, against God, and against evolution. It is the result of immoral values. Immorality is what is causing the low rate of child birth.

The Baby Boom generation invented and created more products, art, and literature than any groups have ever done before them. They put a man on the moon. They invented Tang. They invented Velcro, personal computers, and the internet. They built great cities. They wrote some of the most important musical pieces of all time.

And Baby Boomers used rationalization to justify their actions. But just who do they think that their intelligent, scientific, professional arguments are fooling when it comes to child birth? Not God. Not Nature. Not Evolution. Evolution will not allow a species of any kind to survive if that species does not have enough of a birth rate to at least replace itself.

Evolution will cause poverty and possibly extinction to any species that has too low of a birth rate.

It is so interesting to me that so many people will join the fight to protect specific species of animals like spotted owls from extinction but do not understand how the extinction of a species of man like Caucasians or Jews could be horrible for the future.

It is a surprise to me that so many people are so angry about how American companies outsource work to other nations, but they are not the least bit concerned about outsourcing child birth and raising children to foreigners.

Baby Boomers cannot argue their way out of the punishment for too low of a birth rate and too high of immigration to offset the low birth rate. The punishment just happens. It is the natural effect from immorality and the lack of births. The end game is poverty and extinction.

Ravi Zacharias, a well know Christian Philosopher, said on WGN on TV on March 2, 2014 that the USA is no longer a country of morals. Instead, the USA uses science and professionalism to determine ethics. That decision in itself to replace God with science and professionalism is a moral decision. It allows people to justify their actions by the use of scientific reasoning or professional standards that are ever changing. He went on to say that when people determine what is morality rather than God, then there are no absolutes, there are no morals.

Look at our own Declaration of Independence. If there is no God, no Creator, and no Supreme Judge, then there are no unalienable rights as outlined by our founding fathers. Instead, all rights would be determined by men according to what is politically expedient at that particular time. And if rights are from men, then those rights can be changed by men, therefore our rights would be diminished to political privileges that are granted by the tyranny of the majority, instead of unalienable rights from God.

This is the truth: if there are no children, then there is no future. Without enough child births, the entire society will suffer.

For any group of people, for any species of animals, for any living things: if no children, then no future.

Many people like my friend Paul think that western people are so addicted to life styles and things that they can never return to having enough children. They want so badly to achieve the ever expanding goal called the America Dream that increasing their incomes is much more important than raising children.

Americans of today already have much more than their grandparents. Two cars rather than one car. Central air conditioning. Vacations that fly to exotic places rather than drive to nearby destinations. Homes with multiple bathrooms. Wardrobes with multiple suits, multiple dresses, lots of shoes, etc. Designer this and designer that rather than Sears or Penny's. Computers, smart-phones, Lexus or BMW instead of a Chevy or Ford. Even the poorest of the American society have much more than the middle class of 50 years ago. Yet, our grandparents had an average of much more than 2 children per citizen woman while the current rate per citizen woman is less than half of our grandparents.

If Paul is correct that this birth famine to American citizens cannot be reversed, then those groups of people, races, and religions that have lots of children will eventually replace the Caucasians and Jews as the influencers of the societies in the world.

As said in the Art of War: the largest army will win the war. Wars are not only fought with guns. Many wars are fought in the political arenas. And the largest army will certainly win the war fought in the political arena. Soon, there will not be enough Caucasians and Jews to win any wars ... on battlefields or in politics. The western world will change dramatically because of the attrition of whites and Jews. There will be no more unalienable rights from God. Democracy could be replaced by Sharia Law or socialist dictators like Mao or Stalin or Hitler.

What is worse is that our children are following in our footsteps. They are also not raising enough children. They have been led astray by the examples that they see in their parents. Jesus is quite clear in Luke 16:17 that anyone who leads a child astray will suffer so much that it would be better for that person to put a millstone around that person's neck than to endure the punishment for leading children astray. It is all about karma... karma imposed by God, by Nature, and by evolution. All three (God, Nature, and evolution) promise to punish too low of a birth rate with poverty and possible extinction.

We led our children astray. Abortions on demand for convenience. Infanticide. Divorce on demand. Adultery. Pre-marital sex. Degrading life by making everything more important than raising children. Accepting homosexuality as normal. STDs. HIV.

Just look at what we allow to be taught in our schools, shown on TV, made into movies, discussed in newspapers, and discussed in our homes. We not only tolerate illicit behavior ... we glamorize it and accept it.

There is a big difference between "tolerance" and "acceptance." While it is charitable to "tolerate" others who do those things that are wrong, we should be ashamed of ourselves for "accepting" what is obviously wrong and harmful to our society.

OK, as a compassionate society, we forgive sinners, we tolerate sinners. But that does not mean that we should ever accept sinful actions. It is time for us as a society to take a good look at what we have become as we accept sinful acts as being normal. Look at why God, Nature, and evolution made men and women to be so different from each other. And then explain how homosexuality can ever be "accepted" as normal activity.

In 1 Corinthians 11:28, Paul advised "Let every man examine himself." It is time for us to examine ourselves and what we have allowed to happen to our society.

In "The Four signs of a Dynamic Catholic," published by Beacon Publishing in 2012, Matthew Kelly states the following:

> You should be intolerant of some things. "Relatives" (those that believe that morality is "relative" to time and place and culture) will say that you cannot impose your morality on others, that you cannot legislate your personal beliefs. But if you saw someone beating a child, wouldn't you try to stop that person? By doing so you would be imposing your morality on him or her, but it would still be the right thing to do. Some things are right and some things are wrong, but "relatives" will not concede this... We live in a time of moral and ethical confusion... We have stopped thinking about how we should live and have given ourselves over to living however we want to live.

In John 8:4, Jesus saves a woman from being stoned to death for being an adulterer. Did you pay attention to **all** the words that Jesus spoke to the woman? Or did you just focus on the words where Jesus forgives the woman? Yes, Jesus said that he forgave her for her sins. He "tolerated" her. But he did not "accept" her sins. Jesus specifically said to her to "go and sin no more." Yes, Jesus tolerated (forgave) the sinner ... but he also condemned the sin.

In the 40 years following Roe v. Wade in 1973, the estimates are that more than 60 million legal abortions have been performed in just the USA. If the expected offspring from those abortions are added to the total, then close to 100 million Americans are missing from the population because of abortions since Roe v. Wade. Without immigration, the USA population actually decreased. Isn't it interesting that the immigrants to the USA and their immediate offspring who were born in the USA are about 100 million in the last 40 years? Isn't it interesting that at the current birth rate to white people and at the current rate of immigration, those immigrants will outnumber American citizens in the USA within the next generation?

Do you believe in coincidence? Or do you think that our government knew that the USA was missing a needed 100 million consumers and workers from the lack of child births so it deliberately allowed immigrants to fill those needs rather than correct the birth rate problem?

America, we did it to ourselves. We killed the spark, the innovation, the spring in life that comes from youth in a society. If no children, then no future.

The Kiplinger Letter for Dec 19, 2014 makes some very interesting statements. On page 2, it lists what it believes to be the five toughest issues that the USA faces as a country for the next 50 years.

Three of the five are directly related to the low birth rate to American citizens and the use of immigrants to offset that low birth rate. Here they are:

1. *Keeping our promises to an aging America. Will you and your fellow voters trim future Social Security/Medicare benefits ... or accept higher taxes on yourselves?*

2. *Immigration. Given America's low birth rate, how many more foreign workers will you willingly accept to keep our economy growing, and how will you regulate this?*

3. *Increasing income inequality. Will you accept this trend as unavoidable?*

4. *Environmental protection. How much cost and regulation of your life .... will you accept?*

5. *Your ultimate choice: Bigger government or greater personal freedom.*

For the last several years, the Federal Reserve used artificial financial tools of quantitative easing, printing money, and zero interest rates to augment the declining economy of the USA due to the low birth rate for the last 40 years. Its efforts masked the inevitable results of a low birth rate. The Fed actions artificially inflated stock prices just like what happened in Japan before its economy collapsed around 1990 because of its low birth rate. USA government spending increased to 24% of GDP from 18% and increased the national debt by 100% in just 6 years from 2008 to augment the loss of consumption spending for goods in the economy. Soon, those financial tools will lose their effectiveness. This is a production and consumption problem ... not a financial problem. And the continued use of massive immigration will cause other dire problems. So the only answer is to encourage Americans to breed, breed, breed.

Children are life reproducing itself. Children are the product of love. Children are wonderful. Children are positive instant karma. Children are the products of "the love we make."

In the end, what does it say to you about any society that does not want to have children? Or any society that values things and life styles and careers more than children? Or a society that thinks it can replace people with financial manipulations?

If no children, then no future.

Is it too late? ... It better not be.

Seven

OUR GOVERNMENT CAN FIX THIS.

The USA discourages having children. The tax code discourages it. The government run education system discourages it. Teachers are more interested in teaching our children how to put a condom on a banana rather than teach math and science. The USA suffers from having the lowest scores in math and science of any industrialized countries because of how our teachers are more interested in liberal arts (social agenda) than in science and math. Entertainment glamorizes single, childless life styles more than traditional families. Advertizing convinces people to own more "stuff" and do more "stuff," which are often at the expense of having children. They all encourage young people to live childless lives as adults. Business, entertainment, and government all encourage more immigration rather than tackle the causes for a low birth rate. They are all very short sighted as to what is actually good for America.

In his book, The Demographic Cliff (published by the Penguin Group in 2014), Harry Dent made these comments between pages 300 and 324:

"the Baby Boom generation has peaked in its twenty-five-year Spending Wave from 1983 to 2007and will be saving more, spending less, and paying down debt for years to come. The next generation will not create higher spending and borrowing trends until the early 2020s forward, and even at their peak, the level of real spending will not be as high (because there are not as many of them as are the Baby Boomers because of the low birth rate of Baby Boomers) … All the developed countries are aging and have exponentially rising entitlements obligations … We do not need more fiscal Band-Aids and short term stimulus, which will fade again and again, leaving us with more debt and more "bubbly" markets that will crash again … There is no way that the entitlements can be paid for over the coming decades, as falling births and immigration will make the old to young ratio even higher than economists and world organizations are forecasting … The next downturn will very likely be greater than the one in 2008-09 and will bring a greater crisis … (with more immigration) your culture gets diluted and changed … The borders should be enforced and the illegality made clear."

Both Harry Dent and Charles Krauthammer believe that even China is about to go through a dramatic economic recession because of its low birth rate for the last couple of decades … one child per woman. The lack of births for 20 years that are at least 2 per woman are now causing the number of Chinese in the 20 to 40 year old group to decrease. As that decrease creeps into the group who are over 40 in the next few years, the Chinese economy will falter. On page 352 of "Things That Matter" (published by Crown Forum in 2013), Mr. Krauthammer states that any economist who thinks that the economy of China will continue to grow "overlooks the unavoidable consequences of the one-child policy, which guarantees that China will get old before it gets rich."

Let me propose that our government can implement five bold actions right now that can reverse this low birth rate to American citizens. But will our government do them? It means that our government will risk being unpopular with many voters, especially with businessmen and liberals, so the odds are low that politicians will do anything. But here are the bold 5 anyway:

1. Reform immigration so that all immigration (legal and illegal) into the USA is reduced by 90% to only those immigrants who add specialties to the USA.

Immigration is a drug. It is addictive. It is easy. It is a drug of convenience used to offset our own lack of births. And just like any other addictive drug, too much immigration has horrible side effects.

Right now, between illegal immigrants and legal immigrants along with their offspring who are born in the USA, immigrants add about 1% to the population each year (about 3 million people). Within 25 years (one more generation), with the offspring of those immigrants who are then born in the USA added to the total, immigrants will add more than 33% or more than 100 million people to the total population. As the citizen population decreases from the birth famine, then the immigrants and their offspring will outnumber the citizens of the USA. That is way too much impact on our society… economically and socially. Immigration into the USA, legal or otherwise, needs to be limited to no more than 1/10th of a percent of the total population per year. That allows for assimilation into our society. That would allow about 320,000 immigrants per year.

The first thing that needs to be done to accomplish this is to secure the borders. The next is to reduce the immigration quotas, including H1-Bs, to that 1/10th of a percent in total for only those immigrants that help satisfy specific requirements of the society.

Businessmen and liberals will object. Businessmen want more immigrants so they can sell more products to them and can add more low paid workers to their companies. Liberals want more immigrant voters to help them gain more power. But reducing immigration is the first thing that needs to be done. And then limit those immigrants to those who help the society with skills and knowledge that are needed. America needs to dramatically reduce immigration.

Many businessmen complain that they cannot find enough technical graduates in the USA to fill their needs for scientific and engineering positions. Therefore, they lobby the government to allow more foreign technical people (especially Green Card holders and H1-Bs) into the USA to fill their job openings. They could be correct about not having enough scientific and engineering graduates in the USA. The USA only graduates ¼ of the science and engineering students per capita as in India, Russia, Germany, Japan, and Brazil. Instead, the USA graduates 4 times more liberal arts students and lawyers per capita than any other country. Is there any wonder why the USA is so litigious?

Allowing more immigrants is not a long term fix to the need for scientific and engineering professionals. The USA allowed massive immigration for the last 25 years as a temporary fix at the request of business. 25 years is much longer than a temporary fix. It is time to stop it now and to implement a long term fix. The long term fix is to change the demographics of our college graduates. The federal government should not allow any more federally funded grants, scholarships, or loans for liberal arts degrees. If students want to attend school for liberal arts degrees, then let them do it with their own money. But if a student wants some type of government financial help, then let the government help students who obtain Bachelor of Science degrees ... especially in engineering or science.

Any businesses that employ undocumented workers need to be penalized severely. Businesses will stop employing illegal immigrants and that will reduce the motivation for illegal immigrants wanting to come to America. A reduction in immigration will force the business community to support a higher internal birth rate to increase consumers and to gain lower paid young workers.

Once businesses cannot get more consumers or low paid workers from immigration, then they will get behind a higher birth rate. Commercials will change. Company benefits will change. TV programs will change. Education will change. Tax laws will change. Everything will become pro family and pro child birth. Businesses will cause American attitudes towards child birth to change. And this low birth rate canyon will be cured.

2.   Make the tax laws more family friendly.

The current tax laws do not allow enough deductions to raise children. At less than a thousand dollars deduction for each dependent per year, that does not cover the costs for raising a child. It rewards being single and penalizes having children. So the tax laws need to help those who bring life into the world. My proposal is to allow these deductions per year ... and only these deductions to determine the adjusted income for calculating taxes. A dependent is a spouse or child (up to the age of 22 but not over 22 ... children over 22 need to be treated as adults so they will become adults).

- $10,000 for head of household and for each dependent.
- Up to 10% of total income for charitable contributions.
- Up to $40,000 for interest on mortgages.
- Up to $5000 for education per each dependent and head of household.
- Up to $2000 per each dependent and head of household for out-of-pocket healthcare costs/insurance.

Then determine taxes for everyone as a calculation of a flat tax rate of 35% multiplied against the adjusted income... no other deductions, no progressive income tax, just a flat tax rate on adjusted gross income. The amounts for deductions might be different than these and the amount for the flat tax rate may be different, but the spirit of this is too give a significant tax advantage to those who have children so those families with $50,000 to $200,000 income in today's dollars can afford to raise those children.

As such, a family of 5 comprised of 2 parents and 3 children, with income of $100 K per year and $5 K per year in charitable donations to a church of choice, two children in college at $10 K total plus one child in day care for $5 K, $20 K in mortgage interest, and out-of-pocket healthcare insurance of $10 K would pay nothing in taxes.

In contrast, a single person with income of $100 K, $20 K in mortgage interest, and $2 K in healthcare insurance would pay $27,300 in taxes (27.3%).

A single person working on Wall Street who makes a million dollars a year and only has the maximum deduction for mortgage interest of $40,000 will pay $332,500 in taxes (33.3%).

3. Force the public government employed educators to teach about reading, writing, and arithmetic rather than push their personal

social agendas. Government-paid educators are employees of the government and can be made to do this by the government.

The vast majority of teachers are women and many of them are single. As such, daily, they push their personal feelings on our young impressionable children. At the very time that our children are sponges about everything in life, teachers are promoting life styles that are exactly the opposite of what is needed for a society to have a robust birth rate.

Just as it is wrong for society to push its values on the individual teachers, it is wrong for teachers to lace their personal values throughout what they instruct our children. They are with our children for more waking hours than are the parents. At the impressionable ages of 5 to 15, our children soak up everything that their role models, teachers, put in front of them. And when those teachers glamorize single life styles, homosexuality, and anti-religious bias; then our children learn to be anti-child birth.

Our teachers need to teach subjects, not personal values. This needs to be part of their contracts. At this current time when children pass through schools without knowing how to add, subtract, read, or write; teachers need to stop pushing personal values and start teaching hard subjects more effectively. To do that, the federal and state governments need to change the contracts with the different teachers' unions to emphasize teaching core subjects and to penalize teachers who imbed their political and/or personal values in their curriculums.

And the government employed teachers need competition. Charter schools, private schools, and religious schools will give them that competition. Competition will cause the government teachers to do a better job of teaching real subjects rather than brainwashing our children and grandchildren with their personal values. To get that competition, the tax system must allow for adequate education deductions for alternate education choices when calculating the adjusted income of the tax payer.

Teachers need to put their personal agendas aside and teach our children subjects that help America be a better place. Single life styles do not help America be a better place. Homosexuality does not help America be a better place. The false revision of American History does not help America be a better place. Reading, writing, and math help America. Learning to be good parents helps America.

4. Implement a universal draft.

The Baby Boom generation ran away from serving the country. Viet Nam had a lot to do with that. As such, an all volunteer military was implemented. Therefore, currently, the lowest percent of Americans serve their country in the history of the USA. Many young Americans have no vested interest in the USA. They lack civic responsibility as part of their characters. They live at home much too long without taking responsibility for their own lives, let alone for children. The number of children who are born to families without a father has more than tripled since Roe v. Wade. Many more men feel no responsibility for pregnancy. Being a "dead beat dad" has become normal. Too many young people enter the work force without any skills. Too many young people choose to not enter the work force at all. And the joy of raising children has been replaced by life styles of irresponsible, immediate gratification.

Every person should serve our country. Every person should have a vested interest in America. The highest level of service happened in WWII. The "boys" went off to save the world from the National Socialists (Nazis) and the Japanese while the women worked to support them by making weapons for them in the USA factories. After so much death in WWII, life was cherished as God and evolution and nature meant it to be cherished. When those boys returned home in 1945, the birth rate increased dramatically for the next 10 years. Life was celebrated as the Baby Boom generation was born.

A renaissance is needed. It should be a renaissance of service and life. Every person in America should serve America for a minimum of 18 months when each one reaches 18 years old. There should be only minimal exemptions. Not for gender. Not for race. Not for ailments. Not for education deferments. Not for religion. Only for severe disabilities.

If a young person has not finished high school and if that person completes the draft assignment honorably, then some accommodation should be made to award that person a high school degree, but in no way should the assignment of service to America be delayed. Every person serves 18 months at 18 years old. 18 at 18.

http://en.wikipedia.org/wiki/File:Unclesamwantyou.jpg

Some young people will object to serving in the military. So that those who do not want to serve in the military have an alternative choice for service, each person should be given a choice of the type of service between military and social service. Military service would include all branches of the federal military and National Guard and Coast Guard, etc. Social service would include assignments at hospitals, for government works, at the Red Cross, for government agencies, at police stations, etc. But no matter what type of service, the person must be assigned to a post that forces that person to leave home for those 18 months at 18 years old. 18 at 18.

As such, every 19 year old will have achieved experience at a job. No 19 year old would be unemployed. As 20 year olds enter adulthood, more of them would have a skill, more of them would be confident about leaving home, more would be mature as they enter college, more of them would get married, and more of them would want to raise children, just as it was in the USA before the draft was eliminated.

5. Eliminate all public funding for abortions.

Since Roe v. Wade in 1973, more than 60 million legal abortions have been performed in 40 years. If those children had been allowed to live and create their own children, the USA would have 100 million more "citizens" … and would not need more immigrants.

While the Supreme Court ruled that abortions could not be made illegal, it did not say that the federal government had to financially support abortions. An abortion is elective surgery. So why do tax payers and insurance companies have to pay for it?

Today, the federal government funds abortions in many ways. It does it through funding to Planned Parenthood, by funding to local groups who promote abortion, by requiring that insurance companies provide coverage for abortions, etc. All of this makes abortion a relatively easy and cheap procedure to secure. It also releases men from having responsibility for pregnancy since it's a "woman's right to choose" to get an abortion.

This one item alone drove down the birth rate by actual murder of unborn children and by establishing a mindset that demeans childbirth, motherhood, and fatherhood. And it drove up the number of children born to families without fathers as men abdicated the responsibilities for pregnancy by claiming that pregnancy is a "woman's right to choose."

Even though women have this right to choose an abortion or not, the government should stop taking sides about the issue. By funding abortions, the government is encouraging abortions. By funding abortions, the government has interfered with the First Amendment rights of many Americans. It uses tax money to promote abortions as elective surgery that comes from many Americans who abhor abortions for religious reasons. So the government is interfering with the right to practice religious freedom.

The government should remain neutral on the subject of abortions by eliminating all funding and all government services that sponsor abortions. This one action alone will help increase the birth rate. This one action alone will get the government out of the abortion business. This one action alone will signal to Americans that we as a country, as a society, and as a culture respect life as given to us by Nature, God, and evolution.

In summary, many economists, including Harry Dent, believe that cutting off immigration is too hard for America. They believe that America needs the immigrants to maintain the level of demand for products until America can achieve more births… which might be never.

Product consumption is the issue. Service consumption does not help the economy as much as product consumption does. And as a society ages, it purchases more services and fewer products. It replaces product consumption that has a high economic multiplier with service consumption that has a low economic multiplier. Purchase of a baseball mitt, bat, and ball does much more for the economy than does the purchase of stocks or a payment to a dentist or a payment to a CPA. And economists like Harry Dent do not believe that USA politicians have the courage to do what is needed to increase the birth rate, so they want to continue more immigration to increase product consumption and to provide more low cost employees to businesses. That strategy of more and more immigration hurts citizen minorities (especially black minorities) and women the most.

So the issue is how to increase demand for products until America increases its birth rate to more than 2 per woman citizen. Immigration is one way to maintain product demand …but only one way. And the cost to taxpayers and our culture for immigration is way too much to endure. Just look at Europe to see what happens with too much immigration. And then look at Japan to see what happens with too few births.

During the summer of the 2008 election campaign, a couple of ideas were given to McCain, Palin, and Obama from me to head off the coming recession in 2009. America was not feeling a recession yet, and they ignored my ideas. Those ideas are documented in my first book, Save America Now. One of those ideas from me was how to increase consumption of products made in the USA. The idea was for the government to increase consumption of products made in the USA with components made in the USA that would offset the loss of product consumption as the Baby Boomers grew older than 60 years old. My idea was to have the government cover the consumption gap left by aging Baby Boomers as they aged past 60 without enough 40 to 60 year olds to replace them.

Instead, the politicians chose to bail out banks and the stock market a year later with almost a trillion dollars (it grew to a trillion per year for the last 6 years) that did nothing to increase demand for products. It did nothing to help average working Americans. It did everything to help the top 1% of Americans gain more wealth. And that was even with Democrats in control of the White House and the Senate who claimed to represent working Americans.

The government allowed massive immigration which lowered wages, which took jobs from women and minorities (especially black minorities), and which caused massive increases to government service costs for healthcare, education, crime, and social services. The government tried to stimulate product consumption with massive immigration instead of using the money to buy more products. Again, that was done with Democrats in control of the White House and the Senate who claimed to represent working Americans.

The government implemented the same financial techniques used in Japan of QE, printing money, and zero interest rates with the same results as in Japan. Those techniques failed in creating more product demand and failed at creating full time jobs because they did not create more consumers for products. Those techniques only helped the rich get richer by increasing the money supply for purchasing stocks which drove up the price of stocks ... and by increasing the PE ratio for stocks with zero interest rates which also drove up stock prices. The number of Americans with full-time employment continued to decrease, employment only grew for part-time workers, the growth to GDP remained stagnant, and the average wages per Americans decreased while the values of stocks increased more than 100%.

These charts show stock prices, wages, full-time employment, and GDP. Stock prices increased without any basis to do so other than monetary actions of the government. Increases to stock prices were not justified by full-time employment increases, by wage increases, or by GDP increases. The actions of this government helped stock prices increase without helping the economy. They helped the rich get richer without helping the workers of America. And that was with Democrats in control of the White House and the Senate who claimed to represent working Americans.

Stock Prices:

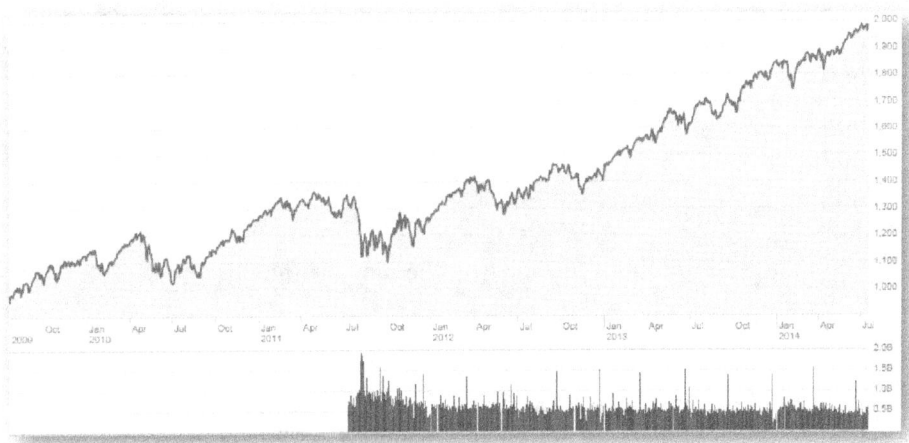

https://client.schwab.com/secure/cc/research/popup.html?path=/
research/Client/Markets/Charts/TearOffChart&symbol=$SPX

Year	Number (thousands)	Per capita income	
		Current dollars	2011 dollars
2012			28,281
2011			28,130
2010			27,968
2009			28,400
2008			28,755
2007			29,682
2006			30,010

https://www.census.gov/hhes/www/income/data/historical/people/

% of USA work force participating in full-time employment.

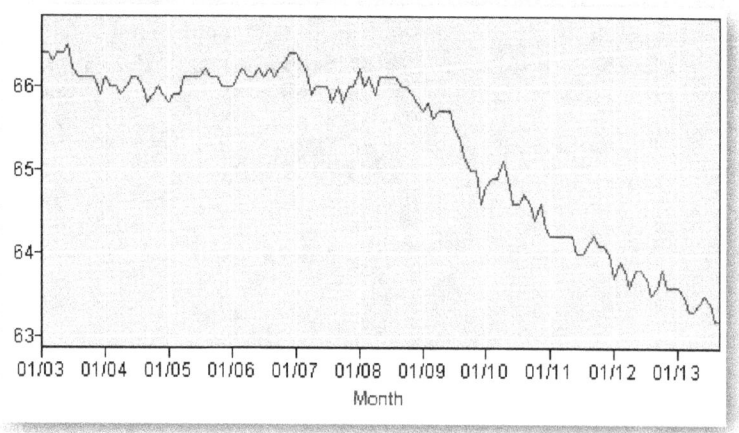

Source: U.S. Bureau of Labor Statistics http://wallstcheatsheet.com/stocks/
how-many-americans-actually-have-a-full-time-job.html/?a=viewall

- GDP growth: 2008-2013: 0.73% (less than 1% in 5 years).
- GDP growth 1Q 2014: - 2.9%

http://www.forbes.com/sites/realspin/2013/04/12/
the-worst-four-years-of-gdp-growth-in-history-yes-we-should-be-worried/

While wages were stagnant, GDP was stagnant, and employment participation decreased; the values of stocks increased 100% … all because of actions by the government. Massive immigration did not help. The government monetary actions only helped the rich get richer. And it all happened while Democrats, those who claim to represent the working class, were in charge of the White House and the Senate.

The depression of the 1930s ended when the government consumed more products for WWII. The New Deal and spending for public works failed. Product consumption for WWII ended the depression. Much like in the solution for the depression of the 1930s, product consumption must be increased to offset the loss of product demand (this time from an aging society). War is a horrible way to increase consumption. So another way to get the same effect of consumption that is achieved with war is for the government to purchase goods made in the USA with components made in the USA and then throw those products away. It needs to consume products just as if it was shooting bullets, making ships, building tanks, or dropping bombs.

For example, the government could purchase 10 million dollars of Harley Davidson motorcycles and throw them in the East River. Well, maybe not in the East River. But if the government gives those bikes away or resells them rather than destroying them, then that did not create any additional consumption or demand … it just replaced existing demand and consumption. The government must buy the products and then destroy them just as if they were used in a war. Crushing them and recycling them are OK. But the government cannot allow those products to be used to satisfy other demand.

It cannot use the money for highways or other internal projects like with the New Deal. That does not create any additional demand for products. The government cannot satisfy pent up demand or other needs by donating the goods. It must consume the products as additional demand in order to add more demand for products to cover the consumption gap of an aging society.

http://en.wikipedia.org/wiki/Softail

For this to work, those products must be made in USA factories with USA made subcomponents. And existing inventory cannot be used to satisfy the government orders. Only newly manufactured products should be allowed to satisfy the government orders.

How much of additional products does the government need to consume? $100 Billion of products per year would do it until the birth rate is fixed. That is less than 3% of the federal budget.

This is unlike Obamacare. Obamacare does not add any consumption of products while it increases costs of a service (insurance) and therefore takes money out of society that could be used to purchase products. This 3% would have a multiplier effect that would actually help the economy.

And the money to do this is readily available by redirecting money from services of the federal government like Obamacare to this project. Services do not have any multiplier effect.

Immigration would not be needed except for political reasons or to provide low cost employees to businesses ... and that harms the wages of American workers while taking jobs mostly from citizen minorities (especially black minorities) and women.

The only real long term solution is to increase the birth rate of Americans. Until that happens, the government should consume products to augment the missing consumption from too low of a birth rate.

Once more, our governments (federal and local) need to encourage more births to American citizens to save America in the long run. They should do these things to increase the birth rate:

1. Reform immigration so that all immigration (legal and illegal) into the USA is reduced by 90% to only those immigrants who add specialties that are needed in the USA. That will force private industry to encourage more internal child birth.
2. Make the tax laws more family friendly. Use taxes to help families with children. Taxes should encourage child birth and penalize childless life styles.
3. Force government employed educators to teach about reading, writing, and arithmetic. Punish them for promoting their personal agendas.
4. Implement a universal draft.
5. Eliminate all public funding for abortions.

What does it say to all of us if the government does not do these things?

Eight

In the End, We are all Dead.

W ell, in the end... yes, in the end ... we are all dead. So what does it matter as to how you live your life? What does it matter as to the condition of the world that we leave behind us? What does it matter if there is enough child birth or not?

http://en.wikipedia.org/wiki/File:Ainhoa_Croix1.JPG

The Birth Famine

If evolution is the only creator of life and there is nothing more than this one life for each person, then nothing matters. In that scenario, everyone dies without anything more after death. So who cares? What does it matter after you die if you were rich or poor or good or bad? It all ends.

But if a God is the creator of life and the Supreme Judge as stated by Thomas Jefferson in our Declaration of Independence, then how each of us treats child birth could make a huge difference in how God treats each of us.

And if Nature is the Supreme Judge, then the future for all of mankind is dependent on how we treat child birth right now.

Yes, children are product of love between two people. Nothing else can demonstrate the love between two people as having children. Not diamonds or gold or a Lexus or a big house or a trip to the Bahamas can show the love of one person for another as does the joy of bringing life into the world. Children are life. Those other items are not. Children are the products of love. Nothing else is. With children, the love between two people is on display just like how a flower is on display as a symbol of the love to the world from God, Nature, and evolution.

So, if in the end it is true that "the love that we take is equal to the love that we make," then what love did we make? What love did we teach our children to make? Did we foster life? Did we make more life? Did we teach our children to love children enough to raise more children of their own?

In the end, did each of us help bring more children into the world to replace us, or not? Did each of us do what is necessary to inspire our society to cherish children so we increase our birth rate?

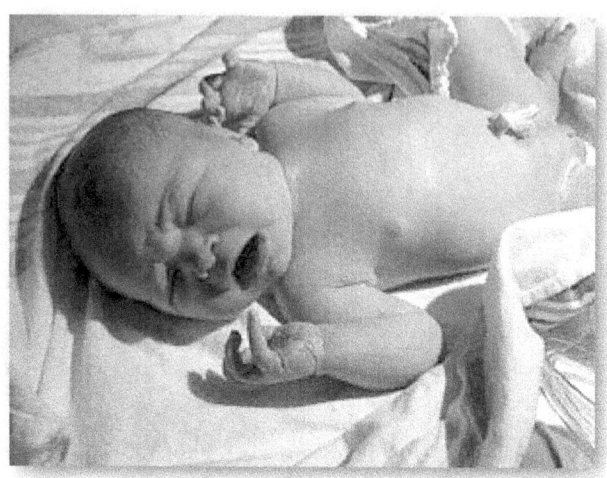

http://en.wikipedia.org/wiki/Childbirth

In her book, "The Tenth" (published by Gated Creative in 2013), Joanne Moudy makes these comments through one of her characters on page 338:

"I knew late term abortions were wrong, but didn't care one way or another about the early term ones… I never gave the subject much thought… The thing that bothers me the most is watching our country move away from morality and into the horrors of Hitler's Nazi Germany or Stalin's Russia. It starts with early abortions, then late term, then getting rid of a new born with defects (infanticide), then older kids, then elderly adults. Anyone who's a drain on society… America used to be different. We used to believe in God. Our laws used to count every life as precious, including life in the womb. But in one singe generation we allowed immoral leaders to erode our society. In doing so, we threw away the value of life, and with it, God."

Who challenged Hitler when he proposed a socialist society void of God? Who challenged Stalin? America is doing the same with its approach to secularism. America is doing the same by forcing insurance companies to pay for abortions and using tax dollars to pay for abortions. America is doing the same by limiting care for the elderly through Obamacare.

We need to determine right from wrong. We need to use those talents that were given to us from evolution, Nature, and God to answer these questions:

Did we make the mistake of encouraging our children to not have children of their own by applauding those people who chose life styles, income, and ownership of stuff that excluded child birth?

Did we praise, idolize, and accept those life styles that extend the birth famine of the Baby Boomers?

Did we accept and justify immoral behavior as being that person's "private" business?

Or did we take a stand in the battle between right and wrong by condemning sin while forgiving the sinner who repents?

And did we do everything possible to encourage Americans to bring children into the world?

Did we do everything possible to teach our children to cherish life as being more important than money, careers, and stuff?

Pope John Paul II: "All human life – from the moment of conception and through all subsequent stages – is sacred because human life is created in the image and likeness of God."

In the end, if no children, then no future.

Works Cited

M uch of the information that is presented in this book is taken from "Save America Now" and "Rules for Conservatives" which were both written by Michael Master. "Save America Now" was published by Dunham Books of Nashville, Tn. in 2009 and "Rules for Conservatives" was published by Dunham Books of Nashville, Tn. in 2012.

The sources of other information were documented in this book as the different pieces of information were presented in the book.

www.ingramcontent.com/pod-product-compliance
Lightning Source LLC
Chambersburg PA
CBHW070553290526
45790CB00002B/664